FRIENDSHIP PRESS · NEW YORK

INTRODUCING Islam

J. CHRISTY WILSON

Foreword

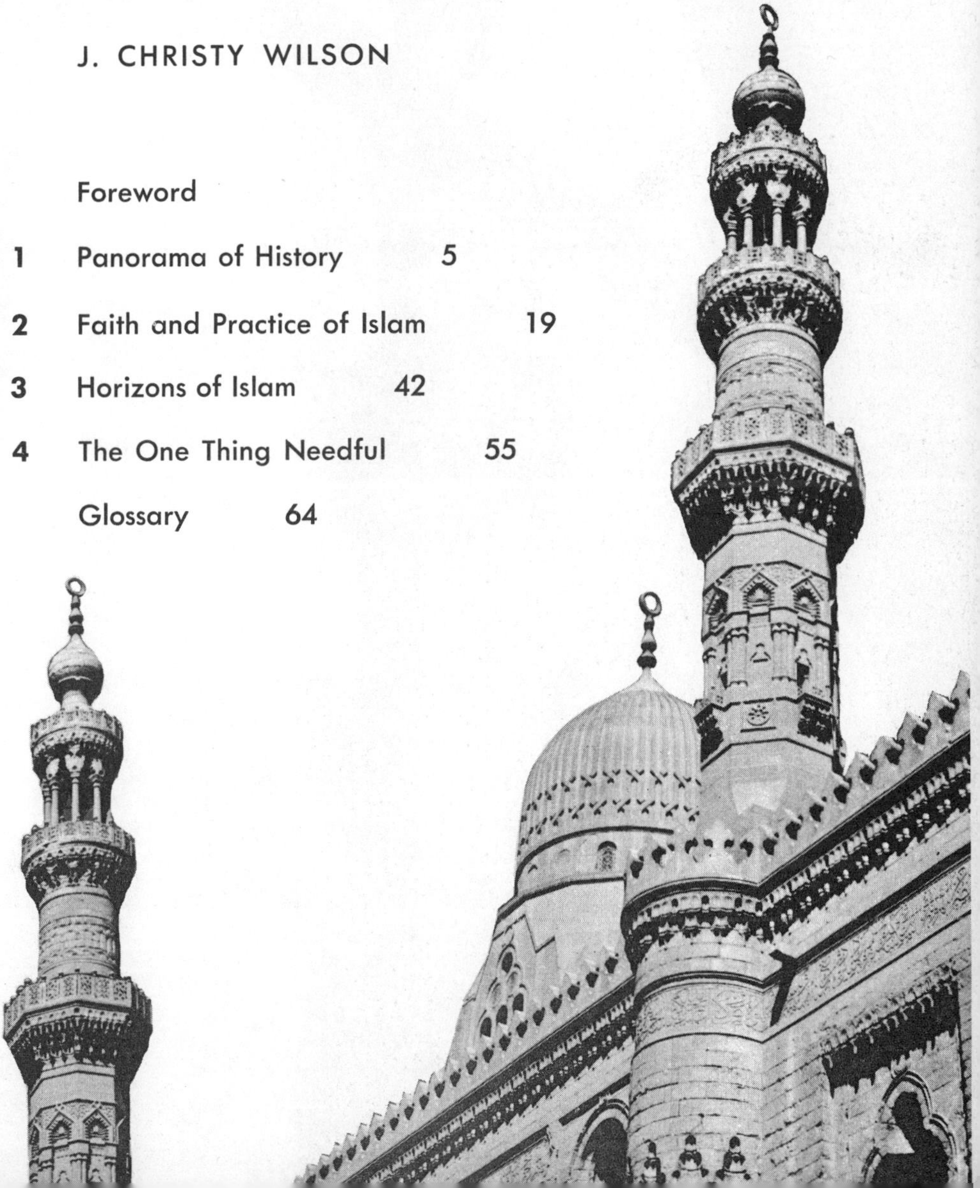

Revised Edition
Copyright, 1950 and 1958, by Friendship Press
Library of Congress Catalog Card Number: 28-763

The mosque is the place of worship for Islam; among Muslims it is the equivalent of the church. Almost always of distinctive architecture and sometimes covered with flashing tile of many colors, the mosque often has a dome over the sanctuary. Frequently the dome is blue, like a reflection of the great blue dome of heaven.

Flanking the pointed arch at the portal of the mosque stand the minarets—tall, slender, and graceful towers. They are characteristic of the skyline in Islamic countries. Five times a day throughout the Muslim world, the muezzin mounts a winding stairway to the small platform of the minaret high above the world and from this vantage point gives the call to prayer.

The mosque and the minaret may be taken as symbols of the religion that we introduce in this book. We will be concerned particularly with an outline of historic Islam and the basic tenets of the Muslim faith. The present world of Islam and recent changes in the Middle East can only be treated incidentally and are more adequately covered in other study volumes. Here we give only a brief review of the history, beliefs, and practices of Islam, going on to glance at its wide geographical distribution.

Although we respect the great truths and high accomplishments of Islam, our perspective could be neither clear nor honest were we not to recognize the unique spiritual values found in Christianity alone. We also record the testimony of some former Muslims as to what they have found in Christ.

An adequate presentation of Islam requires the use of some Arabic terms; we will, however, keep foreign words and phrases at a minimum. An appended glossary defines the Arabic words as well as giving alternate spellings. Because *Introducing Islam* is intended for general reading, we have for the most part used commonly accepted spellings in preference to more scholarly transliterated forms with their Arabic markings.

Let us now take a look at one of the world's major religions.

Worshipers outside the Arabian mosque, Al-Haram Asharif, escape the rays of the sun by crowding one of the porches surrounding the mosque. Supported by carved pillars of the finest marble, these porches give protection from the heat and rain to all observing the Call to Prayer.

panorama of history

The religion of Islam is native to Arabia and bears the indelible imprint of the land that gave it birth. Arabia is a massive peninsula, as large as the part of the United States east of the Mississippi, or in other words an area of about a million square miles. Some have called it an island, for it has the Red Sea as its western border, the Arabian Sea and the Persian Gulf on the south and east, and a sea of desert on the north.

Along the Red Sea and the Persian Gulf are some of the hottest mean temperatures in the world—and mean is the right word for heat that during the summer seldom falls much below a hundred degrees, even at midnight. Yemen, the small country in the southwest, is mountainous and has fertile fields of grain and coffee, as well as grapes and other fruit.

As a whole, however, the picture of Arabia is one of forbidding desert, broken only by the date palms of an occasional oasis. In very recent years oil derricks have spread along the eastern coastline. The black gold from far beneath the ground has brought to this region more wealth than its pearl fisheries ever did, and these were among the most notable in the world.

It was from this land that there emerged, in the seventh century of the Christian era, a faith that has become one of the foremost religions of the world and that has met and conquered Christian populations in many lands. Everyone should know the fundamental facts about so powerful a force in history and in the present world.

About A.D. 570—the exact date is uncertain—Muhammad was born. This child was destined to become the greatest Arab who ever lived and one of the most influential figures of all time. He was born in Mecca, which is about fifty miles inland from the port of Jidda on the Red Sea.

Mecca had been a center of pagan worship for hundreds of years. Here was the Kaaba, a temple and place of pilgrimage, whose famous Black Stone formed the core of the ritual of worship. Here also were many idols, traditionally 354 of them, one for each day of the lunar year.

The people of Arabia at this time included the pagan Arab population, many Jewish tribes, and some Christian groups on the fringes of the peninsula.

Muhammad had a very disturbed and uncertain childhood. His father Abdullah died shortly before the boy's birth. When he was six his mother Aminah took him on a journey to Medina; on the return trip she was taken ill and passed away. The child was then taken by his grandfather Abd al-Muttalib; after two years he, too, died. From that time on, Muhammad was cared for by his uncle Abu Talib.

Though the record of most of his early life is traditional and facts of this period are difficult to verify, it is generally held that at the age of twelve Muhammad was taken on a caravan journey to Syria. There he first came into contact with Christians, and it is said that he formed a friendship with a Christian monk. The period between Muhammad's twelfth and twenty-fifth birthdays may be termed the hidden years in the life of the future prophet of Islam. He no doubt herded goats and camels on the desert, as did other boys of Arabia, and probably went on other caravan journeys.

When Muhammad was twenty-five years of age he entered the service of a wealthy widow named Khadijah. He was faithful in his work and became the manager of her caravans. In this capacity he visited the lands of the north again, going at least as far as Damascus and Aleppo. After some years of devoted service he married the widow who employed him. This marriage gave him prestige and position in Mecca, and though Khadijah was many years his senior they lived happily together.

With wealth at his command, Muhammad was able to take part in the civil councils at Mecca and to have leisure for contemplation. His disposition was deeply religious and he often retired to a cave out in the desert hills to be alone with his thoughts.

Finally he saw a vision in the cave at Hira and felt himself called to be a prophet of the one true God, known in Arabic as Allah—a word closely related to the Hebrew word Elohim, used for God in the Old Testament. The first declaration of his call was to his wife, and she became his first convert. The next believers were his two adopted sons. Then others accepted Muhammad's prophetic mission, the converts including Abu Bakr and Umar, who were to become leaders in the movement.

Ten years after Muhammad had announced his prophetic office, his wife Khadijah died. Within a year, however, he had concluded two other marriages, and new wives were added to the household

Sudanese tribesman. There are at least
seventy-eight million African Muslims.

Short black veils distinguish these women of Qatar, an oil-rich sheikhdom on the Persian Gulf. This type of veil has never been common, and today many women of the countries of the Middle East go unveiled. Only in the conservative, outlying areas do Muslim women still tenaciously cling to the old custom.

as time went by. Among others, he married a woman who had been the wife of his adopted son; another wife was Jewish, while still another was a Coptic Christian. Because of the religious backgrounds of the two last named wives, Muhammad must have had the opportunity to hear Biblical stories in his own household.

The movement he was leading aroused persecution, and a number of the followers fled to Abyssinia. Toward the leader and others who remained, there was still a very strong animosity in Mecca.

In 622 Muhammad made a fateful decision. He left Mecca with his followers and moved to the city of Medina. This migration, or *hijrah,* marks the year *one* of the Muslim era. Muslim years are counted A.H., or after the *hijrah.* The year according to our calendar may not be found, however, simply by adding 622 to the Muslim date, since Muslims adopted the lunar calendar of 354 days.

As has been aptly said, "The flight to Medina changed not only the scene, but the actor and the drama."[1] The Prophet had at first been simply a religious leader who preached the unity of Allah and warned of the Day of Judgment. At Medina his movement grew rapidly and he became not only the spiritual head of a new faith, but also a legislator and a military leader. The change is marked in the suras, or chapters, of the Koran that were transmitted before he left Mecca and those enunciated after he was established in Medina.

The first place of prayer and meeting was the courtyard of Muhammad's own home. The house consisted of a number of rooms of sun-dried brick, with the open courtyard in the center. There were rooms of equal size for each of the Prophet's wives. Houses were also built for his followers.

Around Medina there were watered gardens that supplied the city's five tribes—two Arab and three Jewish. But as the influx of Muhammad's followers increased, there was not enough water for the added agricultural needs. To get supplies it was decided to raid the passing Meccan caravans, since Muhammad had continued to feel a deep resentment toward the people of Mecca who had rejected him. In the second year after the arrival in Medina,

---

[1] "How Islam Arose," by Isaac Mason. Hankow Religious Tract Society, 1936.

a raid upon a large caravan of about a thousand camels produced
the armed conflict known as the Battle of Badr.[1] Though greatly
outnumbered, the followers of Muhammad defeated the forces
of Mecca.

The latter gathered their forces, however, and returned to inflict
a defeat on the Muslims at Uhud in 3 A.H. Muhammad himself
was wounded. The setback was but temporary, as the armed forces
of Mecca did not follow up their victory.

The pattern of conflict had been set, and as the army of the new
religion gained in size, other tribes were subjugated. The Muslims
successfully defended Medina against a siege by the superior
force in 5 A.H. This prolonged struggle is known as the Battle of
the Ditch, from the fact that Muhammad dug large trenches
before the unprotected entrances to the city. There is a story to
the effect that this idea was suggested by a Persian companion of
the Prophet and some credence may be given this statement, for
the technical name by which the ditch or trench was known was
a Persian rather than an Arabic word.

Among the forays was an expedition against the Jews of
Quraizah that resulted, according to some sources, in the killing
of over seven hundred captives and the sale of their wives and
children into slavery. The battles with various tribes continued
through the seventh year after the *hijrah*. That year, however,
under the terms of a truce, Muhammad was able to make the
pilgrimage to the Kaaba in Mecca.

In the eighth year, since there was still hostility in Mecca,
Muhammad determined to attack his native city with an army of
ten thousand men. The Muslims took possession without a battle
and destroyed the pagan idols of the Kaaba, but kept the famous
Black Stone. It is still there—the center of Muslim pilgrimage from
all parts of the world.

In previous years Jerusalem had been the point toward which
Muslims turned in their daily prayers. After Mecca was taken, the
point toward which Muslims faced in prayer became the Kaaba,
and so it has remained.

---

[1] 624 A.D. Early Islamic dates are commonly adjusted to conform to Christian
calendar. This sometimes gives an apparent discrepancy because the Muslim year
is shorter than the Christian.

At first Muhammad had hoped that Jews and Christians would accept his new religion, and it was no doubt a great personal disappointment to him that they did not. He referred to both as "people of the book," and hoped they would authenticate his mission. As he stated in the Koran, "If thou art in doubt about what we have revealed, ask them who read the Scripture before thee." —Sura X:94. In fact, it is very likely that in the beginning he looked upon his own mission as a reform movement and a continuation of the Judeo-Christian religion.

The failure of Jews and Christians to embrace the new faith and the battles that took place in the early years of Islam changed this attitude. The later suras of the Koran show the pattern of hostility toward both Jews and Christians that had been formed by these circumstances.

During the year after Mecca was taken, deputations were sent to various tribes, who for the most part accepted Islam as their faith and its leader as their political head. New verses continued to be added to the Koran.

About this time Muhammad experienced a deep sorrow in the death of his small son Ibrahim, whose mother was a Coptic slave. The child had been named after Abraham, who is known as the "Father of the Faithful" in all three of the monotheistic religions, Judaism, Christianity, and Islam.

The following year Muhammad made the pilgrimage to Mecca in great pomp. The Prophet was now past sixty years of age and the turmoil and rigorous life of the military camp and the desert had taken their toll; he was unwell during the return journey. Back in Medina the illness continued, but from his sickbed he sent out an expedition against the territory that is now the Hashemite Kingdom of Jordan. Although extremely ill, Muhammad went to the mosque for prayers and for a final address to his followers. It is said that he returned to rest his head in the lap of Aisha, his favorite wife. Murmuring, "Eternity in Paradise! Pardon!" he quietly passed away. The probable date of his death is June 8, A.D. 632.

At first there was consternation among Muhammad's followers, but when Abu Bakr heard this, he announced to the gathering crowd, "Whosoever worships Muhammad, let him know that he is dead! But to those who worship Allah, let it be known that he does not die!" The aging Abu Bakr, who had been one of the first converts, became the first caliph, or successor to the Prophet.

Whatever ethical judgments may be made of Muhammad, the man, it is abundantly evident that he was one of the great religious leaders of the world—his influence upon history and the devotion of his hundreds of millions of followers have entitled him to this place. Moreover, he was by far the greatest Arab who ever lived and, judged by his effect upon his own adherents and the world, one of the greatest *men* who ever lived.

The Islamic Conquests

Practically all of Arabia was under the control of Islam by the time of the Prophet's death. In 634 Umar succeeded Abu Bakr as the second caliph. During the ten years of his office the triumphal march of the Islamic state continued. The expansion progressed at a rapid rate and within a century included more territory than the Roman Empire had embraced at the zenith of its power.

A Muslim merchant, one of over 106 million
adherents of Islam in India and Pakistan.

A Syrian sheikh. His desert garb gives no
hint of his nation's rapid westernization.

From Arabia there were simultaneous thrusts against Persia on the east and Syria on the north. In both directions the vigorous Muslim armies met foes who were all but exhausted from their struggle with each other, since the Byzantine Empire and Persia had long been in intermittent and indecisive conflict.

Campaign Against Byzantium. In the Battle of Yarmuk, fought in 636, the fate of Syria was settled by the Muslim victory. Earlier Damascus had been sacked after the Muslim army had made an amazing dash across the desert from Iraq. They were driven off later, only to return to make Damascus the capital of the Islamic Empire. By 634 Jerusalem had been taken after the Battle of Ajnadain. There were some reverses for the Arabs but by 636 Jerusalem was firmly in their control and all of Palestine had fallen to the conquerors.

Persian Campaign. Iraq, an outlying area of the Persian Empire, was invaded in 633, and intermittent warfare continued for several years. By 637 Iraq was occupied as far north as Mosul, which stands across the river from the former site of Nineveh, and as far east as the Tigris River. In this same year (637) the Persian army suffered a decisive defeat at Qadisiya. The Arabs founded Kufa as a military base and surging into Basra, revived that city.

The campaign continued in the provinces near the Persian Gulf, and the ancient city of Susa, in what is now southern Iran, was captured in 640. The great Persian army was finally defeated at the Battle of Nehawand in 641 and the capital city of Rayy, near the site of the modern Tehran, was taken the next year. In a series of campaigns the outlying provinces of Iran were subdued and the Muslims, as the Persians often say, imposed upon them three things: political rule, their language, and their religion. The warriors from the deserts of Arabia had mastered the empire that over a thousand years before had been the strongest power in the world.

North African Campaign. Egypt was invaded in 640 and Alexandria surrendered a year later. For some years, however, the Byzantine Empire made unsuccessful attempts to retake Alexandria and regain control of Egypt.

Advances were made along the coast of North Africa by the Arabs but the conquest of this area was not completed until the beginning of the eighth century. By 711 the Muslims had crossed into Spain and in seven years most of this country had become a province of the caliphate. Bands of invaders began trickling across the Pyrenees into France in 718, but made little progress. In the Battle of Tours, fought in 732, the Islamic armies were decisively defeated by Charles Martel and the threat to all of Europe was averted. It may be noted that the Battle of Tours was just one hundred years after the death of Muhammad.

Mediterranean Region. Sicily and later the island of Malta fell into Muslim hands, but were retaken by European Christian forces in the eleventh century.

At the very close of the century, in 1099, the Crusaders took Jerusalem. They remained in control until Saladin won the Battle of Hittin in 1187. The Christian forces maintained some hold on the eastern Mediterranean until about the close of the thirteenth century, when all the lands fell again under Muslim power. The Crusades were ultimately a failure, since the holy places soon reverted to Islamic control, but they left a tradition of warfare and enmity between Muslims and Christians from which the representatives of the two religions have never fully recovered.

In the campaigns of the Mediterranean lands the Muslims made the greatest conquest of Christian countries in history. Many great churches in this area became mosques and have remained so.

Expansion in Asia. The caliphs of Islam had appointed governors of Armenia as early as the closing years of the seventh century. In 1064 the Seljuk ruler Alp Arslan captured Ani, the capital of this country, which had been the first to embrace Christianity as a national faith.

In the latter part of the seventh and early eighth centuries Muslim expeditions also advanced into central Asia beyond the Oxus River.

No great success was gained in India until the early eleventh century. Then Mahmud of Ghazni conquered considerable territory, and by the thirteenth century all northern India from the mouth of the Indus to the delta of the Ganges had fallen before the Muslims.

In the fifteenth and sixteenth centuries Islam was introduced into Java and soon had very large numbers of converts there and in the neighboring island of Sumatra. It was extended to other East Indian islands, and there are Muslim tribes in the Philippines.

Subject Peoples

In about the eighth year after the *hijrah*, Muhammad introduced a special system of taxation for subject peoples. This plan permitted other religions to maintain their own faith if they paid a tax to show their subjection to the Muslim rulers. They were, however, disarmed and deprived of certain civil liberties and privileges enjoyed by those who accepted Islam. Although there were some groups of Jews and Zoroastrians who were affected, by far the larger number coming under this rule were the Oriental Christians. These have held to their Christian faith throughout the centuries despite disabilities and restrictions.

The Ages of Islam

The spread of Christianity in apostolic times was one of the marvels of history, but the outreach of Islam in its first century was far greater. Islam took all of Arabia first, then the Bible lands

from India to Egypt. Then it engulfed North Africa and finally
Spain. This was due, as already shown, not only to religious and
military zeal but also to the internal deterioration of the great
empires of the period.

By the year 1000 of the Christian era, Islam had come to
dominate the culture of all the peoples in the conquered lands,
except a few tribes, and to set a pattern in almost every sphere of
life. The middle ages of Islam, or the second historic period, is
usually reckoned from 1280 to 1480. During this time the religion
and rule of Islam were extended in Central Asia, Afghanistan, and
further parts of India. It spread across to the great populations
on the islands of the East Indies. During the latter part of the
medieval period, in 1453, Constantinople fell before the armies
of Islam. This era was also marked by the rule of the Ottoman
Turks in the western section of the Islamic empire and the mag-
nificent splendor of the rule of the Mogul emperors in North India.

Clasping the Koran,
Mecca-bound Arab
waits for his flight
at Dhahran Airport.

We may designate the time from the later fifteenth century down to the present as the modern age of Islam. This period has seen the growth of the religion throughout most of Africa. The spread began through the influence of slave traders, followed by other representatives of commerce who were also active missionaries for their faith.

In recent times the propagation of the faith has not been so strongly carried on through lay methods, but the Islamic religion and culture have been accepted by such great masses of mankind and over so wide a portion of the globe that natural increase of population adds millions each year to the followers of the Arabian prophet. Other factors encouraging the growth of Islam are the modernist sects, which, although a small minority of the total, are actively missionary, and the Muslim press, which has become a very strong arm for the extension of Islam and the education of its adherents in the faith.

Politically, the present century has been marked by the break-up of the Ottoman Empire and the abolition of the caliphate. A flood of western influence has poured in to engulf the Islamic world, and these countries now stand at the threshold of a new era.

Table Of Important Dates In The History Of Islam

A.D.

622	The *hijrah*. Migration to Medina, first year of Islamic era
624	Battle of Badr. Victory for the Muslims over forces from Mecca
625	Defeat of Muslim forces at Uhud
627	The Battle of the Ditch, or Siege of Medina
630	Mecca taken by the forces of Muhammad
632	Last pilgrimage to Mecca and death of the Prophet
632-634	Abu Bakr, caliph—father-in-law of Muhammad and one of the first converts
634-644	Umar, caliph
644-656	Uthman, caliph
653	Uthman's recension of the Koran
656-661	Ali, caliph—son-in-law of Muhammad
661-750	Rule of the Umayyad Dynasty (Damascus)
680	Death of Husain at Kerbela
717-718	Year-long siege of Constantinople
732	Battle of Tours. Muslims defeated by Charles Martel
750	Establishment of Abbasid caliphate (Baghdad)
786-809	Harun al-Rashid, caliph in Baghdad, which was a great center of culture and education
869	Malta taken by Muslims
1091	Recovery of Sicily and Malta by Christian forces
1099	Crusaders capture Jerusalem
1187	Battle of Hittin. Saladin defeats the Christians
1203	Muslim rulers in North India
1227	Death of Genghis Khan
1405	Death of Timur Lang (Tamerlane), Mongol conqueror
1453	Fall of Constantinople to the Muslims
1492	Moors expelled from Spain
1517	Beginning of the rule of the Ottoman Turks
1923	Abolition of the Caliphate

faith and practice of islam

chapter two

Muslims of all sects and in all parts of the world are united by the fundamental formulas of the faith known as the Word of Witness, sometimes called the creed. *There is no god but Allah, and Muhammad is the apostle of Allah.* These few words have a remarkably sonorous alliteration in Arabic and are the rallying cry of the faithful among every race and in every clime. There is one God, and one leader of the faithful. The Word of Witness is shouted in the call to prayer at stated periods from before dawn until after sunset. It echoes from mosque and minaret, armies have inscribed it upon their banners, kings use it as a superscription on their coins, it forms an architectural decoration for great buildings and is a wall verse in the most humble Muslim home.

Essential Beliefs

There are six fundamental articles of faith that must be held by every Muslim. They concern: 1. Allah. 2. Angels. 3. Holy Books. 4. Prophets. 5. Predestination. 6. The Day of Judgment.

We will take them up in order.

Allah. The one great accomplishment of Muhammad was the foundation of a religion that holds as an almost fanatical truth that God is one. This has prevented a large section of the world's population from falling into idolatry, atheism, or to any great extent communism, though a number of Muslim governments have been strongly affected by Communist propaganda within recent

times. Since the first converts in Arabia were pagan worshipers of idols, Muslims are justly proud of the fact that Islam has overcome idolatry in many areas.

A beautiful phrase used at the beginning of every sura in the Koran except the ninth is: "In the name of Allah, the merciful, the compassionate," and here we have the basic attributes of a benevolent deity. It should be said, however, that most Muslims will misunderstand and question the statement of the New Testament that "God is love." His power and sovereign transcendence over all creation are so emphasized in Islam that to call him a God of love or to address him as "Father" would be far from Muslim thought. The holiness and righteousness of God are not emphasized as the basis of all his acts as they are in the Old Testament.

Allah is known as the "Lord of the Worlds" or "Ruler of the Universe" and as the "Lord of the Day of Judgment." These phrases are repeated in the stated prayers of Muslims and are found in the first sura of the Koran. This sura is one with which a Christian or a Jew could almost entirely agree, and as a matter of fact, it may be compared to one of the finest of the psalms.

Sign shows Communist influence in Djakarta, capital of Muslim Indonesia.

According to Islamic doctrine, the power and immutability of Allah make him the author of all things, whether they seem to us good or bad, and this doctrine is expressed in many statements of the Koran.

There is a list of ninety-nine "beautiful names" for God that are known to Muslims. It is said that the camel knows the one hundredth name and this is what gives him so much dignity. The common Muslim rosary has ninety-nine beads, or three sets of thirty-three, each bead representing one of the "beautiful names" of Allah.

Dr. Paul Harrison, missionary for many years in Arabia, says of Muslims that he has never known people with such a sense of the transcendence of God and to whom such a belief seems to make so little difference in the common morality of life.

Angels. The second article of Muslim faith is belief in angels. There is a hierarchy of angels, who are reasoning beings and were created of light. Leading examples are Gabriel, who transmitted the Koran to Muhammad; Asrafel, who is to sound the trumpet for the Day of Judgment; and Azrael, the angel of death. Then, there are a great number of angels of lesser rank. Each person has two recording angels to write down his good and evil deeds. There are also two fearsome angels named Munkar and Nakir, who are to examine everyone in the grave after death.

Satan, known as Shaytan or Iblis, was put out of the Garden of Eden when Allah commanded him to do obeisance to Adam, and he failed to comply. (Sura VII: 10-17.)

There are also spirits called jinn, which were created from fire. They may be beneficent but are usually evil and may cause all sorts of trouble. In the English version of *Arabian Nights* and other translated works they are known as genii.

Holy Books. The Koran is considered the last of a long series of books revealed by Allah. It supersedes and to a degree abrogates former revelations. It will later be considered at length. The New Testament, which they call the Injil, is also a holy book and "descended upon" Jesus, but many Muslims claim that the real New Testament was taken back by Christ when he ascended to heaven, and the copy now in the hands of Christians has been changed. The Old Testament or Jewish Scripture is also considered a holy book, or is usually spoken of as two: the *Torah* or *Book of the Law*, and the *Zabur* or *Psalms*. According to Muslim belief many other books of revelation were given to certain prophets but are now lost. The number of lost volumes, however, is stated very definitely as: ten books to Adam, fifty to Seth, thirty to Enoch, and ten to Abraham. There were in all 104 books of direct revelation from God, but only four remain. The *Book of the Law*, *Psalms*, and the New Testament still exist, but in corrupted form, which leaves the Koran as the one authentic scripture for the present world.

Prophets. The fourth article of faith is belief in the prophets. The statement is made repeatedly that 124,000 prophets have been sent to mankind, though no attempt is made to give the names of all.

There are six eminent prophets according to the Islamic reckoning and their names are usually given together with the honorific titles by which they are commonly designated.

1. Adam, the chosen of Allah.
2. Noah, the preacher of Allah.
3. Abraham, the friend of Allah.
4. Moses, the speaker of Allah.
5. Jesus, the word of Allah.
6. Muhammad, the apostle of Allah.

There are some twenty-two other prophets mentioned in the Koran, but many of the greatest Old Testament characters are omitted. Though the other prophets are known and respected, attention has been centered on Muhammad, who is called the "Seal of the Prophets," "Glory of the Ages," "Peace of the World," and two hundred other titles and names.

The figure of Muhammad has been glorified through the traditions and lives of the Prophet written many hundreds of years after his death. Today he is commonly known over the Islamic world, not in the reflection of his real life—quite evident from the Koran itself—but rather as one who existed before the creation of the world, the worker of all sorts of miracles, the ideal character and the sinless one (in spite of the fact that in the Koran he prays for the forgiveness of his sins). Among the more widely mentioned miracles in the later lives of the prophet may be listed the claim that he caused pebbles to talk in his hand, his body did not cast a shadow, he split the moon in two with his finger, trees would bow in obeisance as he passed, and he made a night journey to the seventh heaven (or ninth in some accounts). Some are founded upon references in the Koran and others are entirely without such foundation. Such details of his life as might seem questionable according to the religious code he enunciated are covered by permission or command from Allah, so that any apparent faults of character are transmuted into virtues. Tradition has made the Arabian prophet the supplanter of all former revelation, the sole guide for this life and the effective intercessor on the great Day of Judgment about which he preached.

The traditional stories tell of things Muhammad said and did that form the basis of a set religious code. The Muslim's every act, from morning to night and from the cradle to the grave, is prescribed by this code. There are stated forms for ablutions and purification, eating and the care of the person and clothing, with directions as to almost every act of life. In fact, the law of the Koran has been amplified by the traditions until today Islamic injunctions and rules exceed those of the Mosaic dispensation in the Old Testament.

Among Shiite Muslims[1] great veneration is also paid to Ali, the son-in-law of Muhammad, even to the extent that his name is added to the Word of Witness, making it "There is no god but Allah, Muhammad is the messenger of Allah, and Ali is the vicegerent of Allah." Stories of his exploits that are even more fantastic than those concerning Muhammad are told in the Shiite traditions. There are also lengthy accounts of what the twelve imams, or leaders of the faith, said and did.

The doctrine has become widespread that Muhammad did not inaugurate a new religion but his work was a revival of the true religion, which had become corrupt with the passage of time. This idea is well expressed by a quotation from a Chinese Muslim source. "When our prophet reached the age of forty years, he received the command of God to expound the correct doctrine,

---

[1] See also "Divisions and Sects of Islam," chap. 3, p. 48.

and put a stop to false sayings, and sweep away heresies, and revive again the doctrine handed down from Adam and all the prophets, so he was called the Prophet of the Great Completion. Since Muhammad no other prophet has appeared." [1]

It seems, in fact, that Muhammad himself started out with such an idea but changed his mind after he became master of military and political power following the exodus to Medina from Mecca.

Predestination. The fifth article of faith is predestination, by which is meant the fact that everything that happens, either good or bad, is foreordained by the unchangeable decrees of Allah. [2] It will be seen at once that this makes Allah the author of evil, a doctrine that most Muslim theologians hold. There are many schools that deny entirely the free will of man, while others— including the Shiite thinkers—attempt a compromise doctrine that allows some place for free will.

The fatalistic philosophy of life that stems from this doctrine is all too evident in the daily life of individuals over the whole world of Islam. Even the worst calamities are often accepted with no more than a stoic shrug of the shoulders. This doctrine has also, beyond doubt, had much to do with the static condition and lack of progress in Muslim lands. It is very common to hear educated Muslims themselves say that this is the fourteenth century of the Islamic era and conditions are much the same in the lands of Islam as they were in Europe during the fourteenth century of the Christian era. On the other hand, there has come the strong surge of ideas and modern improvements from the West, so that radio, oil development, motor cars, and air transportation are but the outward signs of a startling era of change in Muslim lands. The result of these factors on the fatalistic outlook of the past is for the future to reveal, but certainly a new era has come to the churning populations in Pakistan and Afghanistan as well as in the lands of the Middle East.

The Day of Judgment. The final article of faith as given by

---

[1] *The Arabian Prophet*, by Liu Chai-Lien; translated by Isaac Mason, p. 299. Shanghai, 1921.

[2] Some authorities would use the term "fatalism," which is indeed a common belief in Muslim countries. Though it differs from the Christian doctrine of predestination, the position of the Koran is rather the determinism of Allah than a fatalistic doctrine.

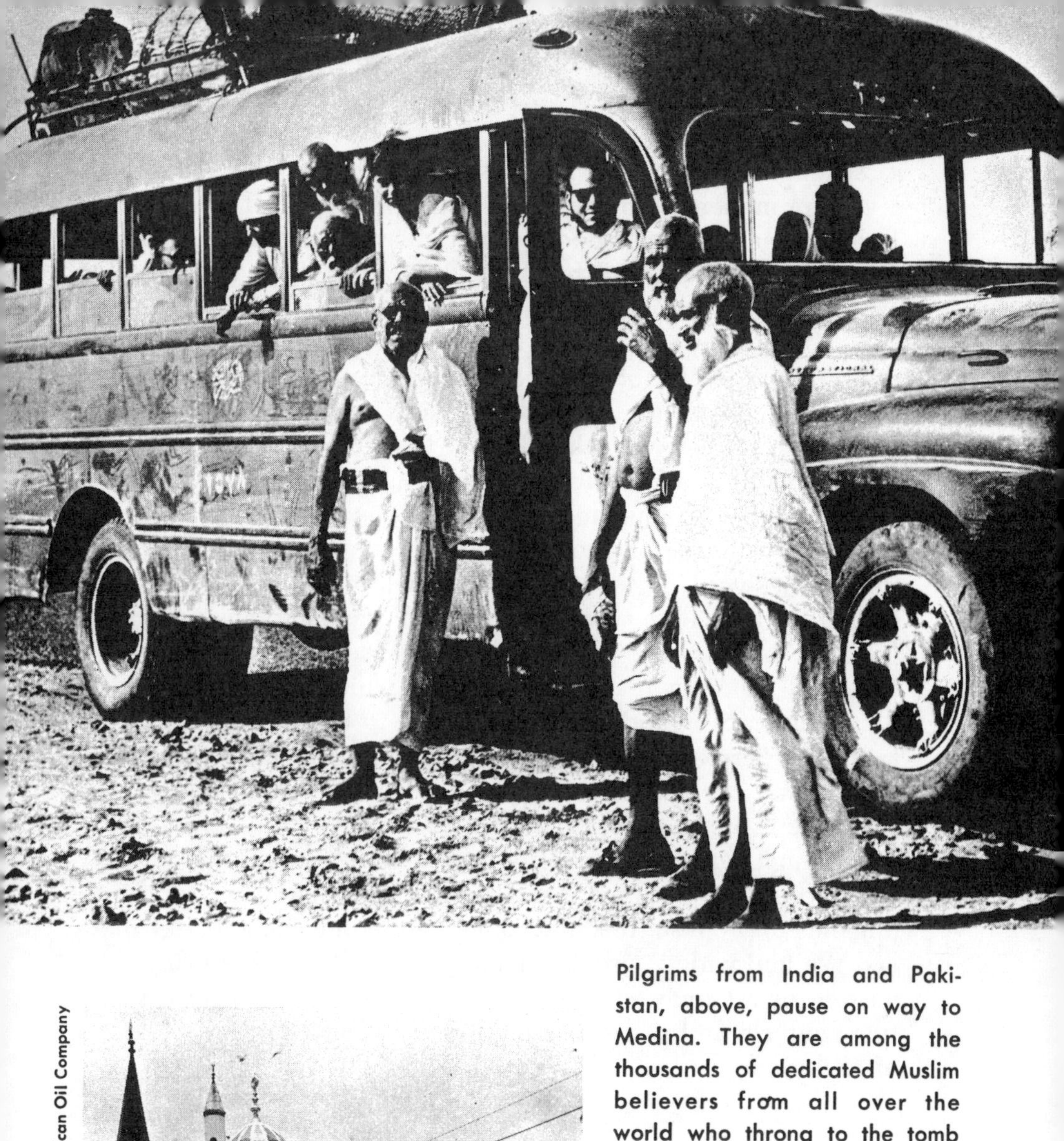

Arabian American Oil Company

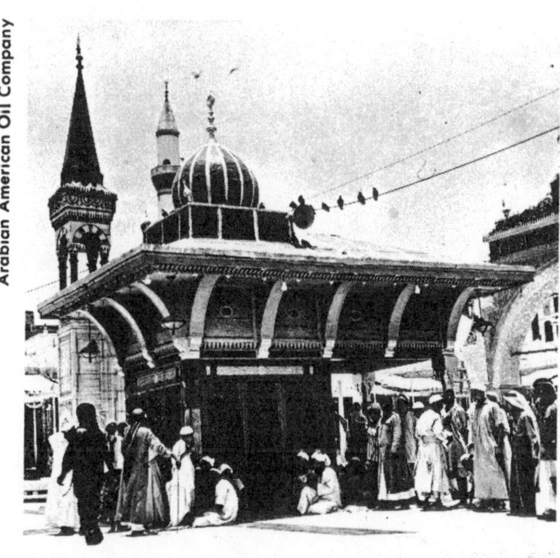

Pilgrims from India and Pakistan, above, pause on way to Medina. They are among the thousands of dedicated Muslim believers from all over the world who throng to the tomb of the Prophet each year.

The Shrine of Abraham, shown on the left, is located in the court of the Great Mosque in Mecca. Known to Muslims as the "Friend of Allah," Abraham is revered as one of the eminent prophets of Islam.

most religious teachers of Islam is the Day of Judgment. This was a very prominent element in the early preaching of Muhammad and remained a central doctrine to the last. It holds an important place in the Koran, and has been developed to an even greater extent in the traditions and theological works of later ages. It is known by various terms, such as the Day of Judgment, the Day of Reckoning, the Day of Resurrection, the Last Day, or the Day of Separation. There are vivid descriptions in both the Koran and traditions of what will take place at that time.

There will be a balance on which the evil deeds of each individual will be weighed against those of good and merit. The soul will cross a bridge of enormous length, as thin as a hair and as sharp as a sword. Those who are evil will topple off into the fires of hell below. Those who are saved will pass across as swiftly as light to the paradise containing the gardens of delight, where there will be every manner of delicious fruits, rivers of wine that do not intoxicate, and beautiful women to be companions of the faithful. There are most graphic descriptions of both the terrors of hell and the pleasures of paradise in the Koran and in the subsequent literature of Islam.

Although fear of the judgment was a decisive factor in early Islam, there has been more and more of a tendency in later developments to promise freedom from all these punishments to believers. We find widely circulated statements like the following lines written by a Chinese follower of Muhammad: "As regards salvation from sin and punishment, the Prophet will save all believers of all time."[1]

The Koran—Sacred Book of Islam

The sacred scripture of Islam is the Qur'an, more familiar to Westerners as the Koran, a book of 114 chapters or suras. The text was transmitted to the Prophet Muhammad in portions of variable length while he was in a kind of trance. It is said that his companions could recognize from certain physical signs when a revelation was about to come. Portions were written on bleached camel bones, stones, palm leaves, and other material, as well as remem-

---

[1] Mason, *Op. Cit.*, p. 301.

bered and recited by his closest friends. After the Prophet had passed away, Zayd, who had been Muhammad's secretary or amanuensis, was commissioned by the Caliph Abu Bakr to collect all the revelations in one volume. He did this, but at a later time many different readings developed and caused endless trouble and discussion. So Zayd was appointed by the Caliph Uthman to make an official text. This document was then sent out to all the principal cities of the Muslim empire and all other copies were ordered burned. The text as revised under Uthman has remained the official one to the present time, though a definite, final reading was not adopted until the tenth century.

According to Muhammad, the angel Gabriel dictated the Koran to him and he merely repeated it word by word. Thus he introduced a doctrine of verbal inspiration of the most mechanical sort. Tradition developed this theory to the claim that the text of the Koran has from all time been inscribed on a great tablet beside the throne of Allah.

In its present form there is a short introductory sura, followed by the longest suras and on to the shortest at the end. There is no logical sequence except according to length, and there is no arrangement either by time of revelation or by content. The speaker throughout is Allah except in the first sura and some passages in which Muhammad or the angels speak. Attempts have been made by various scholars to arrange the suras in chronological order. Although it is for the most part quite evident which portions were revealed in Mecca and which in Medina, yet a complete arrangement in order of time is difficult, if not impossible.

Much of the Koran is in a sort of rhymed cadence that resembles poetry but may still be termed prose. From the point of view of literature, it is considered supreme in Arabic and has no doubt influenced the language to an even greater extent than the King James version of the Bible has influenced English. Being thus the absolute model for literary style and diction, as well as the authoritative pronouncement of Allah, it is considered the one great miracle of Muhammad; in fact, he repeatedly challenged his adversaries to produce anything like it.

To Western readers the text in translation is jumbled and repetitious, and much of it cannot be understood at all. The differ-

This shrouded square building, the Kaaba, is sacred to millions of Muslims throughout the world. It shelters the famous Black Stone that attracted pagan pilgrims to Mecca many centuries before the shrine was turned into a center of Islamic pilgrimage. The Muslims still circle the Kaaba seven times, an ancient rite of the shrine.

Translation of first sura of Koran shows its psalm-like qualities.

ent suras combine laws and legends, prayers and imprecations, as well as numerous stories, many of them concerning biblical characters, yet deviating markedly from the Bible narratives. Scholars hold that a number may be traced to Jewish Talmudic sources and apocryphal gospels rather than to the Old and New Testaments.

It is most difficult for one who is not a Muslim to understand the theory that the Koran was inscribed from all eternity on a tablet in heaven, because some verses supersede and cancel others, and verse one hundred of the second sura says frankly: "Whatever verse we abrogate or cause to be forgotten, we bring a better or its like." There are, furthermore, many references to seemingly trivial matters in the everyday life of the Prophet. Even to Muslims much of the text is unintelligible except through a commentary. Several of the published translations in English have been made by Muslims, in spite of the fact that the orthodox view always has been that the Koran cannot be translated. It is kept with the utmost reverence, only touched after ceremonial ablutions, and read or recited by many millions of Muslims who do not understand the meaning of its Arabic verses. Next to the Bible, it is the most esteemed and most powerful religious book in the world. The Koran is the authority for all Muslim sects and divisions in much the same way that the New Testament is the sacred Scripture for all denominations of Christians.

The Traditions

Second only to the Koran as a source of Islamic law and life are the traditions, called in Arabic *Hadith*. These are records of what Muhammad did, what he allowed, and what he enjoined. As such they form a model for conduct and a basis for law. Every perfect tradition has two parts: first, the chain of names of the persons through whom the report has been handed down; second, the substance of the tradition. These sayings and doings of the Prophet were first recorded by his companions and passed on by them to successors, and so on, through what often becomes a very long list of authorities. Many traditions were of deliberate invention to support the customs or beliefs of rival parties as divisions arose in Islam. The mass of tradition was becoming almost hopeless when about the middle of the third century in the Muslim era the Sunnah or orthodox traditions were codified. Six of these collections were finally accepted, and even these contain many traditions that are contradictory to one another. The selection was made on the basis of authority and content, many thousands of traditions being rejected. The Shiite sect has five separate books, containing not only the traditions of the Prophet, but also records of what the twelve imams said and did.

Quotations from the books of both sects are widely copied and, along with verses of the Koran, are used in architectural ornament and monumental decoration.

The Pillars of Islam

The fundamental religious duties of Islam are five, which have come to be known as the Pillars of Religion, or the obligatory observance on which the faith stands. These are: 1. Recitation of the Word of Witness. 2. Saying the stated prayers. 3. Observing the month of fasting. 4. Giving the legal alms. 5. Pilgrimage.

Recitation of the Word of Witness. The confession of faith, or creed of Islam, is at once the strongest and the shortest summation of belief used by any of the world's religious groups. The two parts of the creed are found in the Koran in different places and, in a stroke of pure genius, were taken out and united. The declaration "There is no god but Allah" comprises but four words in Arabic and establishes the whole basis of theology proper; it makes Islam the third monotheistic religion, the others being Judaism and Christianity.

Although the second part of the creed, "Muhammad is the apostle of Allah" comprises only three words in the Arabic, the whole Muslim doctrine of revelation as well as the rules of conduct and Islamic law of life stem from this basic assertion. A person may

Bedouins of Saudi Arabia observe a period of prayer. Five times a day Muslim believers prostrate themselves in prayer toward Mecca.

United Press International

Islamic lands today show many evidences that they, too, are being drawn into the one-world circle. At the foot of fabled Mount Arafat, site of Mecca pilgrimage ceremonies, modern buses provide sharp contrast to the ancient houses and tents of the Muslim pilgrims....

Evidence of the breakdown of religious exclusivism is seen in the historic meeting of a Roman Catholic Archbishop with Islamic leaders in Cairo....

Care packages for youngsters in West Pakistan demonstrate universal concern for the world's children....

...and a vendor in Mecca offers pilgrims the "pause" that has refreshed millions of North Americans.

Religious News Service

Wide World Photo

United Press International

become a Muslim by the recitation of the creed. It is taught to infants as their first speech, is recited over and over in the five calls to prayer, from morning to night, and on countless other occasions. It is the last word of the dying and is whispered in their ears after the power of speech is gone. The Word of Witness is properly put first among the religious duties, for it is the most powerful formula in the Islamic faith. Down across the centuries and in many lands it has inspired fanatical devotion to Islam.

Saying the Stated Prayers. The five stated prayers are required daily of every Muslim. They are actually periods of worship rather than prayer as we understand it. The worship consists of ejaculations of praise and adoration to Allah. The first sura of the Koran is always included, and other portions may be. The prayers are longer or shorter in accordance with the number of times the set ritual is repeated. It is always the same, but extra Koranic portions may be added, and all must be said in Arabic.

The prayer is preceded by ceremonial ablutions—washing of face, hands, and feet with water, or with sand if no water is available, according to a set form. The worshipers must always face in the direction of Mecca.

The prayer begins with a standing position, the hands beside the head with fingers extended. The other postures are a half-seated, half-kneeling position and prostration, when the toes and knees are on the ground, the hands extended flat beside the head and the forehead usually touching a small "prayer stone," often made of baked earth from some holy place. The half-seated, half-kneeling position is resumed for the conclusion of the prayer. The prayers may be said in any clean place, but are often recited on a mat or rug used especially for the purpose. They may be said at home or outside and individually or in a company of believers (sometimes thousands unite in a great throng). The prayers have added merit if said in a mosque, and especially at the Friday service.

The exact hours at which the five stated prayers are to be said vary in different parts of the Muslim world, but are always preceded by the call to prayer by the muezzin from the mosque or minaret. Recently a loudspeaker has been used in some countries to broadcast the call to prayer. The times are: 1. dawn, before

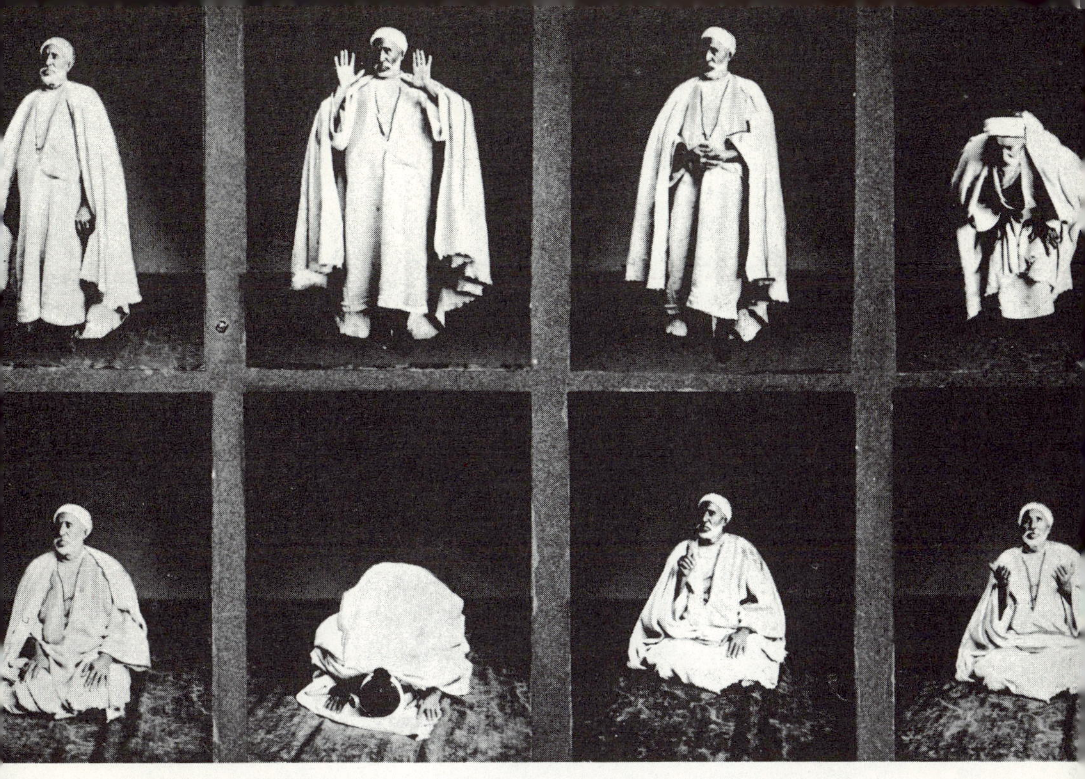

Uniform postures are observed by each Muslim when he prays. From standing, the worshiper continues to a kneeling and then a prone position, as illustrated. Prayer is concluded in a kneeling squat.

sunrise; 2. noon, just after the sun has passed the zenith; 3. afternoon, before sunset—often about mid-afternoon; 4. at sunset; 5. after dark.

Muhammad himself set the pattern for the prayers, which seem in the beginning to have been three times a day. In a Koranic passage there is an apparent reference to a fourth time, but there is no mention of five ritual prayers in the Koran. Just how this number came to be is not clear, although the traditions have many stories about the matter and the observance of five stated prayers a day is now universal among those who follow the sanctions of Islamic law. Within the last generation this ritual of Islam has been neglected in many Muslim lands, where to see a believer observing all of the stated times of prayer or worship regularly seems in many countries the exception rather than the universal custom as it was for centuries.

Observing the Month of Fasting. Fasting is the third pillar of Islamic observance. It is meritorious at all times but is an absolute duty during Ramadan, ninth month of the Muslim lunar year. The fasting is obligatory during the day, but eating is permitted at night. The requirement includes abstinence from drinking water or any other liquid and from smoking. The fast begins at dawn as soon as a white thread may be told from a black at arm's length and lasts until dark when the one may not be distinguished from the other. In most Islamic cities a cannon is fired at dawn to mark the beginning of the fast and in the evening when eating and drinking may begin.

Needless to say there is little sleep at night during the month by those who observe the fast, but sleep is allowed during the daylight time of fasting. More social gatherings and night parties than usual are scheduled during this month. The months rotate around the seasons, since the lunar year is shorter than the solar, so the fast may occur in any season. It becomes an ordeal to those who must work all day in very hot weather without a drop of water or a bite of food. Actual prostrations are numerous, but a person who is ill is not required to keep the fast. In a great many cities the observance is for a large portion of the people only a pretense, though open eating, drinking, and smoking by Muslims is often forbidden by official ordinance. Ramadan was adopted for the fast since the descent of the Koran is supposed to have taken place on the "Night of Power," during the later part of this month.

Giving the Legal Alms. The giving of alms to the poor was practiced and encouraged by the prophet Muhammad and continues as a work of merit. Such charity is distributed at any time of good fortune, on a return from a journey, at a birth or wedding, and on feast days or holidays. This type of alms is voluntary and has caused problems in some places by creating a class of professional beggars. It has discouraged the provision of care for the needy and physically handicapped in social institutions. Though the practice of voluntary charity is widespread, many educated Muslims complain that it is not usually well directed and often tends more to create than to alleviate conditions of poverty and need.

The legal alms that are prescribed by the Islamic code consist of a certain portion of income, the amount of which is determined by a rather complicated system. For instance, one tenth of grain and fruit is required if the land depends upon rain for moisture, but one part in twenty if it is irrigated. From all money received one fortieth is prescribed. There are various additional legal alms on bequests or gifts, on fortune that comes unexpectedly or is not earned. In addition, wealthy Muslims have provided in their wills for bequests of immense sums in gifts and property to pious foundations or for the endowment of philanthropic agencies and religious shrines. Such property has in recent years been taken over by governments in several of the Islamic lands, to be administered by a special department for the benefit of the public.

When Islam held theocratic rule in its early days the alms were collected like taxes in many cases, but in modern times, for the most part, the giving of what is required by the religious law is left to the individual and he may give it to the poor or to a mosque or religious foundation as he chooses.

Pilgrimage. The fifth, and last, of the pillars of religion according to Islam is the pilgrimage to Mecca. This is required at least once during the life of every pious Muslim (unless he is a slave) who is physically able and can afford to make the trip.

The days of the great pilgrimage are from the first to the twelfth of the last month in the lunar year. The three special days of ceremony in Mecca are from the seventh to the tenth of the month.

The ceremonies may be briefly described. The pilgrim before he reaches Mecca goes through a ceremonial ablution and dons the special dress for the occasion, consisting of two seamless tunics. He visits the great mosque and kisses the famous Black Stone, then circles the Kaaba seven times. Three times around are done very rapidly and four slowly. Special prayers are said; the "Place of Abraham" is visited. The pilgrim drinks from the sacred well, Zemzem, and runs between the hills of Safa and Marwa seven times. A visit is made to Arafat, several miles from Mecca. The night is spent there and on the return journey at Mina seven pebbles are thrown at three pillars of masonry known as "First," "Middle Pillar," and "Great Devil." The ceremony is concluded

Outline Of Muslim Doctrine

There Is No God but Allah The Unity of Allah (No other gods, he has no companion.)	1. Creator of all things. 2. Sovereign and transcendent. 3. King of the Day of Judgment. 4. The Beneficent, the Merciful. 5. All things good and bad by his decree. 6. Ninety-nine "beautiful names." 7. Witness and worship required.
Muhammad Is The Apostle *of Allah* Muhammad the Seal of the Prophets	1. Ethics founded on his actions. 2. The Koran: The final scripture superseding all other books. 3. The Traditions. 4. Existence of angels, jinn and devils. 5. Judgment and future life.
Essential Beliefs	1. Unity of Allah. 2. Belief in angels and created spirits. 3. Allah's revelation in books. 4. Belief in prophets. 5. Predestination. 6. The Day of Judgment.
Duties—The Pillars of Islam	1. Recitation of the Word of Witness. 2. Saying the stated prayers. 3. Observing the month of fasting. 4. Giving the legal alms. 5. Pilgrimage.

on the great feast day by the offering of animal sacrifice. After the ritual is over most pilgrims visit the grave of Muhammad in Medina. The pilgrimage may be made at other times of the year but without the same amount of merit.

The number of pilgrims has been mounting of late years; recent figures indicate as many as a million a year, including those from Saudi Arabia. Some thirteen thousand pilgrims came from Indonesia alone in 1957, and Pakistan and Africa are largely represented. Several hundred are usually on hand from China. Many of the better educated Muslims feel that the ceremonies of the pilgrimage were largely taken over from pagan customs before the inception of Islam and tend to compromise the great position of the religion as pure monotheism and its dictum against any form of idolatry. There is not the least doubt that the pilgrimage is a useful institution that brings Muslims of all lands together and sends them back with glowing accounts of what they have seen and done. After the pilgrimage, the one who has taken part bears the special title of *hajj* for the rest of his life. Others than Muslims are not allowed to enter the precincts of Mecca or its environs. Non-Muslims have made the pilgrimage in disguise and written accounts of all that has taken place, but in so doing they have taken their lives in their hands.

The control of Mecca and Medina now lies in the hands of the ruler of Saudi Arabia and was his chief source of income before he began to receive enormous oil revenues. He takes his wives, concubines, and the whole family to Mecca at the time of the pilgrimage each year. Pilgrimage to the other shrines over the world of Islam is very common and is considered as adding merit, though, except among Shiite Muslims, it is but a faint echo of the great pilgrimage.

Recent Practice and Conclusions

Though Islamic law allows a man four wives and any number of concubines he is able to support, polygamy has been limited in recent decades by a growing social conscience against it in higher circles and economic conditions among the common people. Many of the laws of Islam resemble those of the Old Testament, such as the rule of circumcision and the injunction against the eating of pork. The absolute prohibition of alcoholic drinks is unfortunately broken in Muslim countries almost as often as the prohibition law was in the United States. There is no prohibition in Islam against the irreverent use of the name of God, such as that in the Ten Commandments, and consequently the use of the name Allah is extremely common in all sorts of combinations and under many circumstances. Slavery is also permitted and is still in force in some regions.

Many of the greatest Muslim writers and thinkers have attacked the problem of the religion becoming a rigid formalism in which the set times of worship, fasting, and other obligations fail to provide a real spiritual life for the believer. It may be said that the whole Sufi movement is an attempt to avoid the hard theological dogmas and the set formalism of ritual observance. The Sufi doctrine was accepted by orthodox Islam largely as a result of the work of a Persian theologian and writer, Al-Ghazali, known also as Algazel, who died in 1111. He, above all others, was the man who set the pattern for Muslim theology and was certainly one of the greatest thinkers and one of the most deeply spiritual mystics of any time or any religion.

The separation of church and state in Turkey has produced a marked effect upon the rest of the Muslim world. Ali Abd ar Razik, an Egyptian writer of great influence following the first world war, published a very widely read and discussed book, *Islam and the Basis of Government,* in which he upholds the theory that separation of the civil government and religion is truly Islamic, though the opposite has been practiced from the beginning. Despite these elements of modern doctrine the famous remark of Lord Curzon has usually been considered true—that Islam is not a state-church but a church-state. In fact, we cannot fully understand Islam unless we realize that it is not only a religion, but a social and political system as well.

In much of its modern propaganda Islam takes Christendom to task for its recurrent wars, its materialism, its imperialistic politics, and its race prejudice. In Islam, we have the strange paradox of a religion, spread by military conquest and with injunctions to holy war in its basic scripture, becoming the advocate of peace

Syrian pilgrims, protecting themselves against the desert heat with umbrellas, are a familiar sight as they arrive at the Jidda airport on their way to Mecca. Jidda, a Red Sea port in Saudi Arabia, is an important stopover for Islam's many pilgrims.

in a world decimated by wars begun in nations that are nominally followers of the Prince of Peace. The element of truth in the charges of materialism, imperialism, and race prejudice should lead Christians to confession and penitence. Let us also resolve to understand the religious power that unites the whole Islamic world in spite of political divisions; to understand the faith of those who constitute the greatest challenge to Christianity as a world religion, in spite of the notable resurgence of other great religions in recent years.

horizons of islam

Islam is a world-wide religion. Followers of the Arabian prophet are found today on every continent. The countries where Muslims are predominant have been called the great Islamic crescent, but this is cramping the geography of Islam to fit the symbol. More accurately, we should say that these countries form a wide belt that stretches across North Africa and the Middle East, passes down across northern India, and curves to the islands of the East Indies.

Though not a majority, large numbers of Muslims are found in Central and South Africa, in southeastern Europe, in the southern sections of Soviet Russia, and in China, as well as in Burma, Indonesia, and the islands of the South Pacific as far as the Philippines. Islam is also attracting a growing number of adherents in the United States.

Although in many areas accurate figures are not available, we ought to give a brief survey of Muslim populations. With the use of his imagination, the reader should be able to grasp a feeling of the vast distribution and the huge masses of people embraced by Islam.

It is estimated that there are about ten million Muslims in the Arabian Peninsula, where Islam first got its start. Former Jewish residents of this area have emigrated to Israel, and only a few thousand non-Muslims live in the coastal towns.

In Palestine, before its division, the majority of the population was Arab and predominantly Muslim, although some were Christian. With the establishment of the state of Israel, nearly a million Arabs fled to other surrounding countries.

The states of Iraq, Syria, Lebanon, and Jordan have a population of about twelve million. These countries are mostly Arabic-speaking Muslim except Lebanon, which may have a Christian majority. An estimated 98 per cent of Turkey's twenty-four million people are Muslim. The United Nations has recently estimated the population of Iran at about twenty-one million. The majority of the people are Shiites (today, Yemen is the only other Shiite Muslim country). There are some ten to twelve thousand Zoroastrians and a very small number of Jews. The latest figures received from the compilers of the *World Christian Handbook* place the Christian population at less than five thousand.

The 1955 edition of *Annuaire Du Monde Musulman* estimates that there are some seventy-eight million Muslims in Africa. Recent figures give Egypt a total population of twenty-three million, of which one and a half million are Christian Copts. In Somaliland there are over one and a half million Muslims. Ethiopia has over two and a half million Muslims and an estimated ten million Christians, most of whom belong to the Ethiopian Coptic Church. About six million Muslims are found in the Sudan. Libya and Tunisia together have more than four million believers, while Algeria has over eight million, and Morocco contains some nine and a half million. In Nigeria there are some fourteen million Muslims. The balance of the Muslim population is scattered over the whole continent, and even the island of Madagascar has a Muslim population of more than 700,000.

In southeastern Europe there are nearly four million, and it is estimated that the U.S.S.R. has over twenty-one million followers of Islam. Afghanistan has ten to twelve million, Pakistan sixty-six million, and the state of India over forty million Muslims.

There are from ten to twelve million followers of Islam in China (no accurate census, of course), but Chinese Muslims make an over-estimate of up to 40,000,000! Indonesia is another great Muslim center, probably over seventy million. Not in this category, but noteworthy because unexpected, is the estimated (1952) Muslim figure for Australia—sixty-five thousand.

The total Muslim population in the world today is well over

365 million. We should emphasize that these figures have been compiled from several sources and are not in most cases census figures. They do, on the whole, give us a true picture of the enormous growth and importance of Islam in our present world.

Arabic and the Muslim Press

In the Koran, Muhammad repeatedly makes the statement that Allah had given to the then followers of Islam a clear revelation in the Arabic tongue—their own language. Therefore, wherever this religion has penetrated into other language areas, the ritual and the language of worship, as well as the holy book, have remained in Arabic. The stated prayers are not to be said in any other language and, according to orthodox dictum, the Koran is not to be translated. However, there have been translations in many languages and some fourteen have been published in English.

Arabic is a difficult language for Westerners to learn and to speak without an accent, yet it is a wonderfully constructed medium for the expression of shades of meaning and of religious truth. English, on the other hand, is a very irregular language derived from many sources and lacking order both in spelling and grammar. The Arabs are justly proud of their language.

The Arabic script has imposed itself upon a number of the other main languages of the Muslim world. Turkish was written in this script until the adoption of a special form of Roman alphabet between the two world wars. Persian and Urdu are still written in the Arabic script.

Although Islam started as a religion of a single language, its literature appears today in a host of other tongues. There are some important centers of the Muslim press in at least fourteen language areas in the peninsula of India. The Koran and other religious books, and periodicals of all sorts, are published in centers all the way from Peiping in China to Capetown in South Africa. In addition, the modern sects of Islam publish much material in the main languages of the Western world.

Nevertheless, Arabic remains the basic language of Islam everywhere, and whenever a book or tract is published in the Chinese or Indian languages, the sacred key words or phrases are usually printed in the margins in Arabic.

In spite of all this publishing activity, there remains a high percentage of illiteracy among the Muslims. They are quite possibly the least literate, in the aggregate, of any of the world's leading religious groups. It is little wonder, then, that literacy campaigns have been gaining the support in recent times of rulers and governments in Muslim lands. Saudi Arabia, for example, expended 13 per cent of its national budget for education in 1956. This was approximately 400 per cent more than was appropriated the preceding year.

In a monastery at Cairo, the head of a six-hundred-year-old sect receives a visitor. The old man is smoking a hookah, or water pipe.

Islamic Culture

During the first years of the Muslim conquest, the leaders were occupied for the most part in military and political organization. By the time (750) of the Abbasid caliphate in Baghdad they had turned to an interest in culture and the arts. The capital city of the caliphs became the educational center of the world.

The scholars at Baghdad and many other cities copied the classical works of European thought and so preserved them during the period of the dark ages in Europe, later to return the philosophy and literature of Greece and Rome as a gift to the Europe of the Renaissance. But Muslim interest was not alone in the preservation and study of classical literature. They achieved a noted development in theology, philosophy, and science on their own. Medicine became a greatly respected profession, and canons of this and other sciences were so firmly established that they provided the norms for hundreds of years.

It is a notable fact that among the scholars there were many Christians and some Jews. Among those who held the Muslim faith a number of the best known were Persians. When the Arabs emerged to impose their rule upon so much of the world, they did not have a highly developed culture. They did have, however, a tremendous power to assimilate the diverse elements of other cultures, and to contribute the final product of amalgamation to the world.

Islamic art and architecture derived very largely from the countries that were conquered early in the outreach of the new religion. It should be remembered also that the making of any likeness of any creature was forbidden, so that painting and sculpture were cut off at the source. However, certain peoples, notably the Persians, never did fully accept the dictum against the reproduction in art of animals, birds, other creatures, and even human or angelic forms. This can be noted in their miniatures and rugs, as well as other types of artistic expression.

To appreciate Islamic art we should first of all realize that Eastern art has little in common with that type of Western art that attempts to picture things as they are actually seen. In style it is somewhat closer to ·Western experimental art, but whereas the latter is aimed largely at interpreting reality through new

The Taj Mahal, supreme achievement of Muhammadan art,
was built by Shah Jahan for his favorite wife, Mumtaz Mahal.

forms, Oriental art depicts an ideal or fairy-like world of the imagination. Conventional concepts of perspective are not accepted, so that surfaces look all out of place and crooked unless one understands that perspective is definitely rejected in favor of showing the design on a surface, or a rug, or the details of a mosaic. Islamic art seeks for fineness of line, for color harmony, and above all, design.

With the prohibition of the representation of figures, Islamic art turned with great intensity to design. The term arabesque has become common in English to designate a design of interlacing lines and figures that produce a pattern of intricate beauty. The designs are used for such widely separated purposes as the embellishment of books or the decoration of great buildings. The Arabic script lends itself in a remarkable way to such decoration. The art of calligraphy was even more highly developed because of the rule against portraying natural objects, and quotations from the

Koran and other symbols were adapted to architectural decoration in some of the most beautiful buildings the world has ever known.

It was probably in the development of architecture that Islamic art and culture reached their zenith. The Arabs had in their native land at the emergence of Islam no monumental architecture. Their buildings were for the most part of sun-dried brick, with the trunks of palm trees as supporting pillars. They found, however, an architectural tradition with ages of development in Egypt, Syria, and especially in Iran. By combining elements from these ancient cultures they developed an Islamic form that is still one of the wonders of the world. Striking examples of this form are the Alhambra of Spain and the Taj Mahal[1] of India.

Whether the building be of finest marble and decorated with semi-precious stones or covered with shimmering colored tile faience in a harmony of beautiful colors, the high pointed portals, the minarets, and domes combine to make one of the most beautiful architectural forms of the world, and beyond doubt the most decorative. Yet all is accomplished with the essence of reserve and good taste.

Divisions and Sects of Islam

There is a tradition to the effect that Muhammad predicted that his religion would be divided into seventy-eight sects and only one of these would represent the true Islam. As a matter of fact the total number of denominations or divisions in Islam has gone far beyond seventy-eight, but of course each sect claims that it is the only true Islam.

The largest division is between the Sunnite and Shiite branches of the religion. The former is orthodox Islam and is strong in Arabia, North Africa, and the Mediterranean lands, as well as being the vast majority in Pakistan, India, China, and Southeast Asia. The Shiite division has the majority in Iran and Yemen, many adherents in Iraq, and several million in Pakistan and

---

[1] Though the Taj Mahal is quite on the model of earlier Persian buildings and was the combined design of several architects, it is still Islamic in form and is judged by many to be the world's most beautiful building.

northern India. The Shiites are the ones who broke away from the original organization, and may be called the Protestants of Islam. They do not accept the first three caliphs as true leaders with the sanction of Muhammad. They believe, rather, that the true line continues through Ali, the fourth caliph, who was the son-in-law of Muhammad, having married his daughter Fatimah. Ali and his eleven descendants make up the twelve imams of the Shiite sect, though a branch of this division, the Ismaili, accept only seven of the imams. Both the Sunnites and Shiites base their faith on the Koran, but have entirely different books of tradition. There are many differences in ritual and belief that need not be mentioned here. But as an example, it might be noted that a Sunnite or Shiite Muslim may be spotted at once by the way he performs the ablutions before the stated prayers; the one will wash his hands up to the elbow, the other from the elbows on down to the finger tips.

In the second and third centuries of the Islamic era several codes of law were compiled on the basis of the Koran, the traditions, consensus of opinion among the learned, and deduction from the other sources. Four such codes were eventually recognized, and orthodox Muslims may be followers of any one of these schools of legal interpretation.

Islamic theology has made so much of the transcendence and power of Allah that he seems distant and unapproachable. In fact, Islam by absolute logic would probably lead to deism, or the idea that God created the universe, wound it up like a watch, and set it aside to run itself. But there is something in the soul of men everywhere that leads them to a longing for fellowship with God, and this has produced in Islam one of the strongest movements in its religious development. This great movement, which has been termed Sufism, tends toward the opposite extreme of deism, and almost, if not quite, leads to pantheism, which sees the deity in everything. The Sufi is the supreme mystic of Islam. Sufis may be found in almost every quarter of the globe where Muslims live. The dervish orders are among the groups of mystics. They have become known in the West by some of the peculiar practices that certain orders adopt, such as the whirling dervishes who spin round and round until they sometimes lose conscious-

Learning the Koran, two Libyan boys recite by rote, repeating the words on the cardboard until the quotations are thoroughly memorized. The man is their teacher.

ness. The dervish is a religious mendicant, but the orders have acquired a great deal of property, which includes meetinghouses and hostels.

Many of the most noted among the Persian poets have been mystics and in the rare beauty of their verse have contributed the element of mysticism to Islamic literature. Consider, for instance, these lines from Sa'di, one of the most read and quoted of Persian poets:

> God of one essence formed the race of men,
> So all are members of one body, then.
> If any member cause some pain or ill,
> The body as a whole must suffer for it still.
> You, who the thought of others banish from your mind,
> How can you yet deserve the name of humankind?

Most authorities would consider Al-Ghazali, a Persian of the eleventh and early twelfth centuries, as the last truly great theologian of Islam. His work was done in Nishapur, in Iran, which was also the home of the poet Omar Khayyam, and later

The new Islamic Center in Washington, D.C. This beautiful Center affords a worship place for Arab officials and Muslim visitors.

in Baghdad and Syria. He may be classed as one of the leading philosophers and mystics of the world. He was a great admirer of Christ, and it is in the Sufi mysticism that Islam and Christianity approach nearest to each other at the spiritual level.

It remains for us to mention the modern sects of Islam, which are in general considered heretical by the orthodox body of the faith. Principal among these is the Ahmadiya movement, which began in 1879 at Qadian in the Punjab. It has divided into two groups that differ primarily in the interpretation of their founder's claim of prophethood. Both have adopted the principles of propaganda and extension that they have seen in use by Christian agencies, while at the same time they keep up a strong attack on Christianity. Their fundamental dissimilarity from orthodox Islam is in an interpretation of the faith by Western rationalistic methods and a modernist view of many doctrines, such as their contention that holy war should be a spiritual conflict, not actual military attack. A part of the varied missionary work of both groups has been the translation and publishing of the Koran in parallel Arabic-English editions. There is a mosque at Woking, near London, and literature is published in several European countries, as well as at Lahore.

Something over a century ago a movement arose in Iran that was called Babism. This later became Bahaism and has spread to America and the West. It has adopted doctrines from both Christianity and Islam and has a modern veneer of rules and regulations of its own. It has become a separate religious movement and so may not be reckoned as a sect of Islam in this day. It was, as a matter of fact, banned from the land of its birth in 1955. The group has built a large and charming temple of unique design at Wilmette, just north of Chicago.

Chicago, as well as other parts of the United States, has attracted another sect that terms itself "Muslim." Statements by the leader of the movement, however, show that he does not seem to have much of an understanding of the real meaning and code of Islam. This sect has made considerable headway among Negroes in the United States and has a publishing center in Brooklyn, New York. Activities of genuine Muslim groups have shown an increase in recent years, also. A beautiful mosque has been built and dedicated in Washington, D. C., and there are Muslim meeting places in Detroit and other cities. An attractive magazine is published in California and a number of tracts are distributed from this center. These latter groups in the United States do not necessarily represent new sects so much as new activities, and their work could well have been included in the paragraphs dealing with the outreach of Islam. Accurate figures of growth in the Western hemisphere are not available.

A modern movement of a conservative nature is that of the Wahhabis in Arabia. This is a return to the fundamental Islam of Muhammad and the Koran and is noted because the leaders of the movement have been those who controlled both the pilgrimage to Mecca and the oil concessions of Saudi Arabia.

The Modern Look

In the few years since the Second World War practically the whole Muslim world has gained self-determination in government and political independence. Thrown into such responsibility in the atomic age, without the evolution of centuries that took place in Europe and the West, many states where Islam is the predominant religion have faced vast problems and new areas of responsibility and experience.

For about thirteen centuries the caliphate was considered absolutely necessary as one supreme head to bind all Islam together. The present century has seen it abolished with no strong demand for its re-establishment. In the United Nations assembly an "Arab bloc" exerts a powerful influence and Muslim nations have formed alliances to stand together. They also show a great deal of independence however, and nationalistic feeling runs very strong in each of the newly independent nations.

The Middle East has become extremely important from the political point of view and communism has been quick to recognize this fact and has done much about it. The longest Russian frontier—and what might be termed its vulnerable under side— lies along the borders of Islamic states from Afghanistan and Pakistan on the east to Turkey on the west. From events in Egypt, Syria, and other parts of the Muslim world the West may no longer take for granted that Islam is in itself a safe buffer against communism in the Middle East and South Asia. Communism may not have so much effect in Arabia, the home land of Islam, where the rulers are fabulously wealthy from oil revenues, but its propaganda has been especially strong in Pakistan and Indonesia, the two most populous Muslim states, and also in India, which has the world's largest "minority" problem in its forty million Muslims.

From the time that Turkey was declared a modern secular state in 1928 there have been tremendous changes following hard upon each other and the pace of progress toward the new era has been greatly accelerated since World War II. Several of the Muslim countries have adopted new codes of civil law and this has superceded the Islamic religious law in most areas of life. The former dominance of ecclesiastic rule, and of the mosque over education has been almost entirely broken and most of the new universities in Muslim lands are co-educational. All the states are passionately endeavoring to build up modern educational systems.

In Egypt there has been a real campaign for "woman suffrage" and there are feminine contingents in the army. Pakistan, Iran, Syria, and Indonesia have granted women the right to vote. In fact one of the most striking features of change in the past twenty-five years has been the emergence of women to take an increasingly important part in commerce and industry, education, government service, and even politics. The abolition of the veil in Turkey, Iran, and other states marked a new era for women in Muslim lands, and also for men who had formerly been deprived of the refining influence of women in society.

Although the present generation has progressed rapidly into the modern world, there remain massive and tremendously difficult problems in the Islamic lands. To overcome the poverty, ignorance, and disease, which are largely the results of the fatalism and inertia of past centuries; to move from a feudal economy into a socially responsible modern state demand the finest qualities of leadership. However, as Kenneth Cragg has remarked: "When discontent succeeds apathy there is a new dimension." Such there is today in the world of Islam.

With many of the educated younger people in Muslim lands there is a tendency to emphasize the cultural and national aspects of their faith rather than phases of religious dogma. They are not for this reason easier to approach with Christian truth, for they are no less ardent; rather they are stronger in their support of other parts of their religious heritage.

In closing, we glance back to recall that Islam has spread over much of the globe and today controls the lives of hundreds of millions. It is not only a religion, but a political, social, cultural, and economic system as well. With all of its many divisions and sects and all the races and languages represented, there is still a great unity in the whole world of Islam. Indeed, it may well be described as one of the most cohesive systems known to man.

Upon this universal body of Muslims, powerful new forces are impinging in our day. There has been a notable departure from the religious sanctions of Islam among educated people in several of the Muslim countries. Secularism, materialism, and communism are making their impact. Islam and the Middle East are in a fluid state. Which way will they turn?

the one thing needful

Considered from the Christian missionary standpoint, Islamic lands are undoubtedly among the most difficult fields of the world. In addition, they have been relatively neglected by the Christian church. In fact, had Arabia not been early by-passed in the preaching of the good news in Christ, Islam might never have come upon the stage of history.

Muhammad took the Arabian tribal organization, to which each member owed absolute devotion, and enlarged it into the brotherhood of Islam. Islam is considered one body and no member is allowed to leave the body any more than a finger, for instance, could leave the physical body. If any individual does break away, the body considers this member dead, and in addition the body suffers by the loss. The apostate who openly renounces Islam is breaking what are regarded as the most sacred ties of family, tribe, nation, social and economic system, and religion. When he denies the faith of his fathers he brings upon himself social ostracism and is branded a traitor to his nation. The complete loyalty demanded of individuals explains the almost absolute cohesion of an Islamic group. Freedom of religion is an idea foreign to Islam.

From the human standpoint, the work of a few Christian missionaries in the Muslim world seems hopeless indeed, if success in mass conversion is held to be the criterion. The outlook for the Christian church in Muslim lands is quite as hopeless as the outlook for the few disciples who, without organization or financial or political backing, faced the paganism and the power of the Roman Empire. The task is as hopeless as was that of William Carey when he first went out to India, or Robert Morrison when he went to China, or John G. Paton when he went to the islands of the South Seas. Yet, who would deny the mighty results of these men? They began and carried on their task in the power of God—not their own.

In a similar way the effect of a few Christian missionaries in Muslim lands in the past century has been outstanding. They were pioneers in education over all the world of Islam; they started the first hospitals and introduced modern medicine and surgery; they trained the first nurses in these lands. Christian missions have cared for and cured those suffering from leprosy. They have carried on great campaigns of relief and have served people of all races and creeds in these countries, in the name and in the spirit of Christ. More important than all this, through the preaching of the gospel, Protestant Christian churches have been founded in practically every Muslim land. Members of these churches are relatively few, but they constitute a foundation, and to build upon it they need the continued support and fellowship of Christians in other countries.

The ancient Christian churches in the midst of the Muslim world, such as the Gregorian Church of the Armenians, the Church of the East (Nestorian) of Iran and Iraq, and the Coptic Church of Egypt, as well as other ancient Christian groups under Muslim domination, have maintained their faith and life through all the centuries with a remarkable tenacity—and often by the witness of martyrdom in terrible numbers. These Oriental Christian churches holding a minority status and under the ruling Muslim states have built up, by their mere resistance, a solidarity and cohesion almost equal to that of Islam. From the beginning of the modern missionary movement, missions in various areas have made efforts to help those ancient communions toward a real spiritual revival and in recent years there has been an encouraging response among groups in these churches.

Although the number of converts from Islam who have taken the great adventure of faith, daring to confess Christ openly and join the church, has been relatively small in the primary Islamic countries, some of these converts are truly wonderful characters who are writing by their lives the modern *Acts of the Apostles* for the world of Islam.

From years of friendship and fellowship with many of these heroes and pioneers of the faith who have left Islam to accept Christ, we have learned that they made the momentous decision because they found in Christ spiritual realities that were not in Islam. He came to mean more to them than life itself. It would be well to mention several of them, in order to learn of their conversion in their own words; to measure the price they had to pay for their faith.[1]

Years ago in Tabriz, a city of northwestern Iran, there was a remarkable man in jail. His name was Mirza Ibrahim, and the accusation against him was that he had become an apostate from Islam. The Crown Prince of Persia then lived in Tabriz and, having heard the story of the man in prison, he called him before the royal presence. The Prince, who was also governor of the province, said: "Mirza Ibrahim, I have heard your story and I admire your courage, so if you will do the Namaz (a Muslim prayer) here before me, I shall not ask you what you believe, but you will be released; you will be a free man."

The prisoner took a small Gospel from his clothing and testified in a wonderful way. "I know that your Royal Highness has the power of life and death over me, but I have found in the Gospel my Lord and Savior Jesus Christ and new life in him. Nothing that you could possibly do could take away from me that new life I have found in Christ. On the other hand, I could never deny my Lord by doing the Namaz. I can not do the prayer; I am not a Muslim."

He was put back into prison and a few days later he was strangled by other prisoners. Mirza Ibrahim found Christ and knew that He was both a perfect example for life, which Islam does not have, and a living Lord who gives to his disciples a new life of beauty and power. Today, there are some two hundred mosques in the city of Tabriz. There is one Protestant Christian church. That church is the true monument to a man who was

---

[1] For more stories of these converts see *The Christian Message to Islam*, by J. Christy Wilson, New York, Fleming H. Revell Co., 1950.

John A. Subhan, Methodist bishop of India. Formerly a Muslim of the Sufi sect, he is now widely regarded as a power for Christianity in his homeland.

willing to give his life in testimony to the Master who had given his life to redeem this convert from Islam. The blood of the martyrs is the seed of the church, and it is little wonder that these churches God is calling out of the Muslim lands have iron in their blood.

John A. Subhan of India was formerly a Muslim and follower of the Sufi or mystic type of Islam. He became a Christian. His pilgrim road led him to membership at one time in the Roman Catholic Church. He is now a Methodist bishop and a power for Christianity in India. He testifies of what Christ means to him:

In accepting Christianity I have accepted the leadership of One who is able to change life and give strength in weakness. He enables me to overcome things which mar and destroy life, and gives peace in my heart and grace to live victoriously, and grants the right of citizenship in heaven. I find that Christianity is Christ, and that to be a Christian means to live in his fellowship, so that when faced with temptation and assailed on every side by the rising tide of doubts and despair or grief, it is enough to look into his face and yield all to his safe keeping, and he does the rest. My manifold needs met by his manifold grace. . . . When tempted to bad temper I can draw on his patience, when to harsh judgment on his gentleness, and when to impurity I can make his dazzling purity my shield and shelter."[1]

A young mullah of Islam in Senna, a city of western Iran, came, as the result of reading the Bible and contact with a Christian evangelist, to a spiritual crisis in his life. He tells of it thus:

One night I was very miserable during prayers in the mosque. Realizing my sin I went home and fell in the dust of the hallway. I prayed to God to guide me to the truth, as he was the Savior of the lost. Then I went back to the study of the Bible and the Koran. After four months of such study the light broke in upon my soul. I can never praise him enough.

This young man had a brother who waited for days with his rifle at the Roman Catholic Church in their home city—not understanding the difference between Protestant and Catholic —planning to shoot the new Christian whenever he attempted to enter the church. Because of this error the young man escaped to the mission station in Hamadan. He studied medicine in the hospital there and later in England. After he had become a noted physician, Dr. Sa'eed Khan Kurdistani preached in the mission church of the capital city, Tehran. Of this he says:

I was able to speak for Christ to the prime minister and to the leading men of the country. Dr. S. M. Jordan asked me to preach in the church, but I asked if he did not think it too soon. He replied that all knew I was a Christian. So I prayed over it. I think I was the first convert from Islam to preach in that church. The utmost I can say is that the Lord Jesus Christ loved a great sinner. He saved a brand from the burning and he loved me to the end in spite of all my sins and failures.[2]

Parenthetically, the brother with the gun was converted and became a Christian.

---

[1] *How a Sufi Found His Lord,* by John A. Subhan. Lucknow Publishing House, 1942.
[2] For an account of his life, see *Dr. Sa'eed of Iran,* by Jay M. Rasooli and Cady H. Allen. Grand Rapids, Mich., Grand Rapids International Publications, 1957.

The penetrating spiritual insight of Dr. Sa'eed Khan Kurdistani had comprehended the fact that despite the elaborate ritual of Islam, he had to come to Christ for forgiveness of sin. The realization of just how forgiveness was possible in Christ came to this convert long after his conversion, and his deepening love for Christ was reflected in his own life until he came to be known as the "beloved physician of Tehran."

The Bible has brought other such people to a personal discovery of Christ, but none of them have been as colorful as Mansur Sang. A pedlar, and sometimes medicant, he traveled back and forth over most of the countries on the eastern Mediterranean and on to Iraq, Iran, and southern Russia. During his travels, he found a New Testament and, having much of it read to him, he learned many passages by heart. Over a period of several years he became a devoted Christian, and everywhere he went—over desert and mountain, on foot or by caravan or bus—he became a burning evangelist who preached the gospel by word and deed. He distributed thousands of Gospel portions and tracts and made his own way by selling simple medicines and pulling teeth in villages where there were no dentists. Finally he passed away in one of the mission hospitals. The brass seal that he used everywhere to sign his name was a witness to his faith. At the top was his name, Mansur Sang. In the center was a cross, and below "Slave of Christ."[1]

Years ago, a Muslim woman remarked to an American woman missionary, "Your prophet, Jesus Christ, has done so much more for you women than our prophet has done for us. If Jesus were our prophet how we would love him." A woman named Homai who could not read became a Christian, and when asked the reason she replied, "If I were lost in the desert and came upon two figures, the one a dead man and the other living, from which one would I ask the way? Now we know that Muhammad is dead and we visit his grave in Medina, but Christ arose from the dead and so I want to ask the way of life from him."

---

[1] See also the account of his life in *New Voices, Old Worlds,* by Paul Geren. New York, Friendship Press, 1958.

These references show how converts discover the following unique features in Jesus:

1. They find in Christ a perfect example.

2. He gives them a perfect ethical code for life.

3. They find in him forgiveness for sin and freedom from its guilt and power.

4. Through the Holy Spirit they receive power for a new life of love.

5. They find peace and power in the fact that Christ rose from the dead and so gives assurance of life eternal.

6. Above all, it may be, they see in the Cross not only the universal symbol, but the center and soul of Christian truth.

On this last point a voice comes to us from Afghanistan, practically the only country in the world that never had resident Christian missionaries and has remained consistently closed to the gospel (until recently, when a church was established in Kabul). Yet Iqbal Ali Shah from Afghanistan, who was educated in England but never became a professing Christian, has come to understand the meaning of the Cross more deeply than many who profess Christianity. He says:

The Cross is the center of all revelation. Have you ever thought what the Bible would be like without the Cross? Take the Cross out of the book and you won't be able to recognize it. If there be no promise of the Cross in the Old Testament, then its laws distress me. It is a book of fatalism. If there is no Cross in the New Testament, then it blazes with pitiless splendor. But put the Cross back, and at once the book becomes a Gospel. Its law becomes love; its shadows flee away; its destiny is the Father's house.

To reveal my sin merely would load me with despair, to forgive my sin merely would make me afraid of tomorrow. I want my sin conquered; I want to get it beneath my feet. The Cross is the place of victory. Christ did it upon the Cross. I say it reverently: he could not do it but for the Cross. It was expedient for one man to die for the people. He had put away sin, all sin—original sin and actual sin—by the sacrifice of himself. "There was no other good enough to pay the price of sin. He only could unlock the gate of heaven and let us in." Education could not do it. Social reform cannot do it. Our beautiful essays and ethical sermons

Road from Mount Arafat permits bus trip from Jidda to Mecca in hour's time. The forty-five mile run was a hot, wearisome journey for pilgrims a few years ago.

cannot do it. It is Christ upon the Cross who discovers sin, who forgives sin, who conquers sin.[1]

Since these great spiritual facts are unique in Christ, they are to be found through the instrumentality of no other person and in no other religion. As the Apostle Paul felt that he was constrained by the love of Christ to preach the gospel in Damascus, Jerusalem, Antioch, and throughout these lands of the Book, so we feel today this same high duty and privilege.

Various gatherings have been held of late years between Christian and Muslim leaders in a friendly spirit to seek a better understanding of the respective faiths. What was formerly known as the "great Muslim controversy" is a thing of the past and Christians now endeavor to present Christ positively. They avoid argument or criticism of Islam, believing that when the love of Christ reaches into the hearts of people—he wins them.

As we study the essentials of Islam and think of the global extent and great power of this religion, may we as individuals and the church of Christ as a whole be moved to attempt the strategic task of winning the Muslim world to faith in the true Savior of all the world, not by force of arms or by power politics,

---

[1] Quoted by Samuel M. Zwemer in *Evangelism Today*, p. 23, New York, Fleming H. Revell Co., 1944. Used by permission.

The historical well of Zem-zem from which the faithful drink. Said to be over four thousand years old, it has been equipped with faucets only in recent years.

but by a great spiritual campaign of love. Jesus does not want political power, but does want the hearts and wills and souls of all these people in the Middle East and the whole world of Islam.

We repeat for emphasis the importance of the Word of Witness in Islam. *There is no god but Allah, and Muhammad is the apostle of Allah.* Missionaries to Muslims have pointed out that the Christian also has a Word of Witness. These words came from the lips of One who had a far greater effect upon history than any other person who ever lived—and all his influence has been for good. The Christian Word of Witness is found in John 17:3.

> *And this is life eternal*
> *that they might know thee the only true God,*
> *and Jesus Christ whom thou hast sent.*[1]

The second and third clauses very much resemble those of the Muslim Word of Witness. The essential part that has no parallel in the Muslim statement is the first clause *"And this is life eternal."* After all that *is* the difference. Christ alone is life—abundant life, life eternal.

---

[1] King James version.

glossary

Arabic. A Semitic language from the same group as Hebrew and Syriac. The language of the Koran and the stated prayers.

Caliph. The religious and political leader of Islam after the death of Muhammad.

Hājj or Hadji. One who has made the pilgrimage to Mecca.

Hijrah or Hegira. The emigration of Muhammad and his followers from Mecca to Medina, from which date the Muslim chronology begins. The year 1 of the Muslim calendar was A.D. 622.

Imam. An Islamic religious leader or saint, also a leader of services in a mosque; of particular significance to the Shiite sect.

Islam. The name its followers give to the religion founded by Muhammad. It is from a root meaning "surrender." It denotes surrender of the person to Allah.

Iran. The country called by the Greeks Persia, but it has been known to its own people from ancient times as Iran; the name deriving from the same root as Aryan.

Iraq. Known to the Greeks as Mesopotamia, the land of the two great rivers, the Tigris and Euphrates.

Kaaba or Ka'bah. The small building in the court of the Great Mosque at Mecca, which contains the famous Black Stone. The Kaaba is the center of pilgrimage and worship, and the point toward which all Muslims throughout the world turn in prayer.

Qur'an or Koran. The sacred book of Islam. The entire volume is a little longer than the New Testament.

Muhammad or sometimes Mohammed. The name of the founder of Islam.

Muslim. Derived from the Arabic participle of the word Islam; it means a follower of this religion.

Muezzin. The one who shouts the call to prayer at stated times during the day from mosque or minaret.

Shiite or Shiah. One of the sects of Islam founded by followers of Ali, the fourth caliph, who was the husband of Fatimah, daughter of Muhammad.

Sunnite or Sunni. A member of the orthodox branch of Islam and by far the largest division to which belong most Muslims of Arabia and the Mediterranean countries, as well as a majority in India and the East.

Sufi. A mystic of Islam. Many of the great scholars and poets held to this mystic interpretation of the religion.

Sura. A chapter of the Koran.